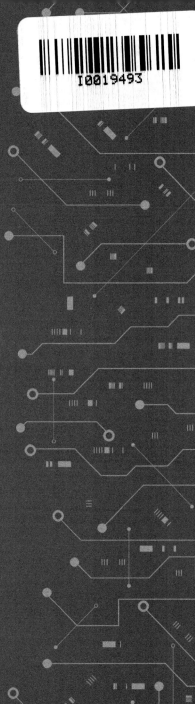

I0019493

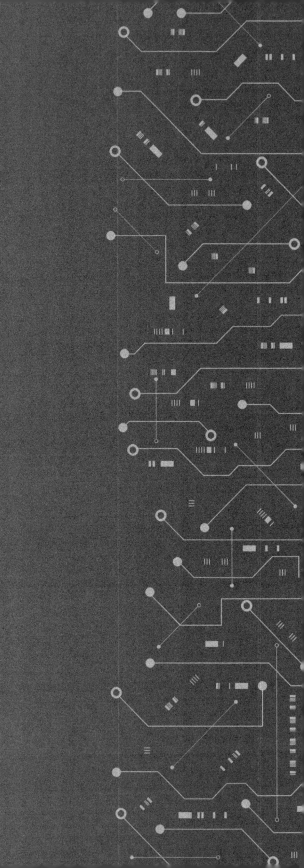

C++ PROGRAMMING

A STEP-BY-STEP BEGINNER'S GUIDE TO LEARN THE FUNDAMENTALS OF A MULTI-PARADIGM PROGRAMMING LANGUAGE AND BEGIN TO MANAGE DATA INCLUDING HOW TO WORK ON YOUR FIRST PROGRAM

ALAN GRID

TABLE OF CONTENTS

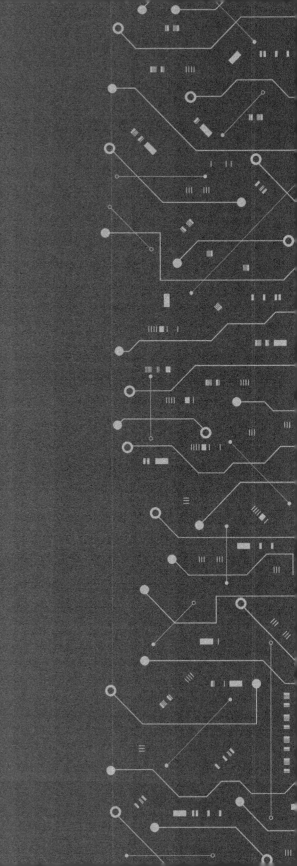

INTRODUCTION

There may be a lot of different coding languages, and C++ is not usually on the list when it comes to easy coding languages that we are able to work with along the way. We may find that there are a ton of benefits of working with this kind of language, but it is often seen to be a bit harder to work with compared to some of the others out there.

As we are going to explore throughout this guidebook, you will find that this is actually a really great language to work with. It is going to provide us with some of the best tips and tricks that we need and will show us how to actually write out some of the different codes that we need inside of this language. If you are looking for a coding language that is powerful, that can help with web applications, games, and so much more, and you want to learn how to use it today, then this is the guidebook for you.

Inside, we are going to learn everything that we need to know about coding in the C++ language. We will start out with some of the basics that come with working in this language, such as what this language is all about, some of the benefits of working with this language over some of the others that are out there, and a look at some of the history that is going to come with this language.

Once we have some of the basics down of the C++ language, you can then move on to some more of the things that we need to explore as well. We will take some in-depth looks at the syntax and the basics that come with this language. It is a bit different than some of the other coding languages out there, so it is important to learn how to make this happen, and then work on our codes from there. We will also explore some of the different libraries that are popular and work well with the C++ language that can extend out some of the functionality that we are able to see with this kind of language.

At this point, we have some of the basics of coding in C++ down, and we know a bit more about this language as a whole. It is now time to actually get into the information about how to do some of the coding that we want. There are so many different types of codes that we are able to focus on, and many different things that we are able to work within this language, and we are going to look at what these are, the codes that work with them, and so much more.

We will end this guidebook with a look at how we are able to do some of the basic debugging that is needed in this kind of language. There are times, especially as a beginner in this language, when the codes are not going to necessarily work the way that you would like, or there are going to be errors that you need to fix. This can be difficult for a beginner because they want to be able to handle these codes and get the programs to work, but they may be uncertain as to how to fix some of the mistakes that are made.

What is C++?

A lot of beginners categorize C++ as a complicated programming language. Whatever the reason it may be, C++ is not a complicated language but a computer language that is with a lack of good resources for beginners. This is the way it is because it is a programming language that has evolved from another major programming language (C programming language) for the past four decades.

"C++ is a programming language that is a spinoff to C programming language with the addition of Object-oriented principles such as inheritance and polymorphism. C++ is a subset language of C that evolved into a much bigger instance that it is intended to be."

History of C++

In the initial days, C++ is just used as a fork language for C and is used to be converted back to C before compiling as there is no direct compiler. A compiler called Cfront is famous for doing this job. However, after a few years, people working with C++ have found it too difficult to create code in a language that doesn't have an actual compiler. So, certain developers started developing a compiler, and the task is finally achieved by Bjarne Stroustrup with a working C++ compiler.

With the implementation of strict syntactical structures within few years, C++ has been recognized by ISO (International standard organization) in 1998. The first updated version was released in the same year, and people were surprised by the new additional features that C++ started to offer. It has started using advanced turing techniques to decrease the compile-time and has also introduced templates in the first version. All these robust new features have helped C++ to develop complex software that supports system programming. Within a few years, C++ has improved tremendously and has included a lot of advanced features that can be used to create generic applications.

It is important to appreciate Microsoft for the sudden up rise of C++ as a programming language. Microsoft started to use C++ for its development software Visual C++. A lot of programmers developing applications for Microsoft systems started to find how reliable and comfortable C++ is to work with. By 2009, C++ standard library has been updated with various complex systems, mathematical and time functions.

Why has C++ become successful?

The success of C++ is mainly due to its object-oriented nature. In the early 1980s, the object-oriented programming paradigm took the technological world by storm. People were impressed with the adaptability and simplicity it offers. A lot of built C libraries at that time can be easily transformed into C++ functional libraries.

All of these factors combinedly helped C++ to become one of the popular high-level programming languages of this decade. It is estimated that by 2025, 15% of the Robotic applications will use C++ as a primary language to develop their resources.

Setting up a C++ environment for different operating systems

All of the software that is used to create C++ software consists of a code editor and an inbuilt debugger to show possible errors. If you are an old cliched guy, you can simply use a text editor and run the program using the command-line environments. It still works perfectly. However, for this section, we will discuss advanced integrated development environment software that can be used to create C++ programs.

How does the IDE work?

IDE's use the combination of the editing program, Compiler chain mechanism, and debugging to create efficient programs.

Note:

Remember that C++ doesn't provide an interpreter if you are trying to work on the command line execution program.

C++ is famous among programmers for its advanced capabilities and easy syntax. Even with the impact of high-level programming languages such as Java and Python, C++ does not lose its charm. This chapter, a comprehensive introduction to C++ programming language and its history, will help you understand the importance and origins of one of the popular programming languages in detail. In this book, we have explained various complex programming topics in Layman's terms. To understand and appreciate much of the information, it is important to understand the importance of C++ as a programming language. Let us learn in detail about C++ now.

What is special about the New C++ version?

The newer versions of C++ are developed to support developers who are trying to implement complex real-world projects. Here are some of the notable advanced features that C++ provides.

a) Advanced data structure implementation

Simple data structures such as Tress and Linked lists can be easily implemented through basic C++ versions. However, it is impossible to implement advanced data structures such as graphs and binary trees using the older versions. Newer C++ versions, on the other hand, provide standard libraries that help us to implement map and hash values which can be further used to implement advanced data structures.

b) Cryptography features

The newer versions of C++ provide dedicated libraries that can be used to implement complex cryptography features in both web and mobile applications. These libraries can also be used to create software that deals with ciphers and stenography.

c) Lambda implementation

Lambda implementation is essential to run data science and machine learning applications. For example, contemporary deep fake software use C++ rendering libraries that are built using lambda expressions.

d) Advanced Object-oriented features

We all know that C++ is an object-oriented language. The basic versions only support single inheritance, whereas the newer versions can provide multiple inheritances to your projects. With the newer versions, we will also be able to use multiple operating overloading and complex polymorphism features.

CHAPTER - 1

HOW TO WORK ON YOUR FIRST PROGRAM

Once you have downloaded the C++ environment that you would like to use, we are going to start right in with your first code. The code that you would have to use to make this work includes the following:

```
#include <iostream>
using namespace std;
int main ()
{
court << "Use This One!";
return 0;
}
```

You have a few options available when it comes to writing this out. You can choose to write this out in your compiler, which will be available in your environment, or you can choose to write it out and save it to your computer. The second option is sometimes nice because then you have the code saved and could copy and paste it any time that you would need it in your code.

Either way, you should carefully consider the type of text editor that you want to work with. Most of them are going to be device-specific, so you need to look for the one that goes well with your particular computer. Some of the options that you can go with are Windows Notepad, vlm, vl, Brief, and EMACS. If you would like to have an editor that is compatible with more than one platform, then the vlm and vl options are the best ones to choose.

When you write out your own codes, you should write them out in the text editor first to get a rough draft on the program, and then you can move them over to your compiler later on. This makes it easier for you to check your work and avoid mistakes with the code that you are currently working with.

C++ compilers

Just like with the text editors, there are many compilers out there that you can work with. The problem is that while you do get a lot of choices to pick from, many of these compilers are pretty expensive. That is because most of the compilers that you will come across are meant for elite hackers who have mastered what was in the other lower-level compilers, and now they want to make sure they can take it to the next level.

The good news is that there are some compilers that you can get for free. You just need to be careful and watch out, just make sure that you are getting ones that are good and will have all the features that you are looking for. One compiler that works out well with C++ and can be good for a beginner to use is GNU. It is best when used with the Linux systems, and you may already have this one on your system. To check whether the GNU compiler is available on your system, use the following code:

```
$ g++ -v
```

Basic syntax

The C++ language can be defined as a program that will use objects to help keep everything organized and will allow the code to communicate and complete other functions using various methods. There are four important parts that come with the C++ language and these include:

- Classes

These are the organizational tools for your language. They can be seen as boxes that can hold onto or store objects and will sort out similar ones. You can label your class anything that you would like, but it is good coding practice to place objects that, in one way or another, have similar characteristics into the same class.

- Object

Objects are things in your code that have states and behaviors. These could be things such as colors, texture, shapes, and so on. You will usually classify these objects into classes that have similar objects. So, if you had a class that was about dogs, you may put the different types of dogs in that same class.

- Method

This is a term used in coding for behavior. There can be as many or as few methods as you would like to work with. This is how you can manipulate the data, and actions will be played out based on the method that you are working with or using. Without using the right method, your program won't know exactly what it's supposed to do.

- Instant variable

These refer to the individual objects that you are working with. Each one is classified using a unique set of variables that act like the fingerprints to identify your object. You can use some values to assign the right variable to the object when you create it.

And that is the basics of writing a code in C++. You should take some time to write out the code above in your compiler to gain a little bit of practice to understand what it is that you should be doing here. We will have a look at some of the things that you can do with these codes later on, but this is a great place to start.

The C++ Data Types

Just like with some of the other coding languages that you may want to work with along the way, there are going to be quite a few data points that show up in your code as well with C++. You will often be working with variables, for example, which are just going to be spots that you reserve in the memory of your computer so that the different parts of the code will stay safe. There are a lot of data points that we are able to focus on when it comes to working in the C++ language, and these will include:

1. Boolean

2. Double floating point

3. Floating point

4. Integer

5. Character

6. Valueless

7. Wide character

The C++ Functions

We also need to take a look at some of the functions that are going to come up when we are working with the C++ language. A function is pretty simple and is just going to be a group of statements in order to perform a task. Each program that you want to write out in C++ is going to have a minimum of a function, which can be known as the main() function, but it is possible that you will need to add in some more functions to get their code to work the way that we would like.

You will be able to do this in a number of different ways. First, we have the option of choosing to divide up our code so that it is in several functions based on what we would like o see it work. How you decide to dive up the code and how many functions you use will depend on you, and what you are trying to write out on your code. But most programmers are going to dive it up in a manner so that each function is going to work on his own task.

A function declaration is going to tell the compiler about a function name, the parameters that come with the function, and the return type that we are going to see. Keep in mind though that the definition that we are going to see with the function though is going to be found in the actual body of this function.

The standard library that we are going to see with the C++ library will be able to provide us with numerous functions that are already built into the program that we are also able to call up any time that we want. For example, if we are working with the function for strcat(), it can be used in order to help us to concatenate two strings. Then we are able to work with the memcpy() to help us to copy one location of our memory over to another one. These are just a few of the different types of functions that you are able to work with, and you will find that each of them is going to work out in a similar manner.

With this in mind, we need to take this a bit further and actually see how we can apply the function in C++. The code that you will be able to use in order to define the function will include:

```
Return type function name (parameter list) {

Body of the function

}
```

These function definitions will consist of a function header and a function body. The parts of the function will include the following:

- Return type: The function that you are working on may return a value, and you will use the value of return type in order to get something to return here. Some functions will be able to do the operations that you want without returning value to you. With the syntax that we used above, you would end up with an answer to the void.

- Function name: This is the name that you will give to the function. When you add in the name of the function with the parameter, you will get what is called the function signature.

- Parameters: The parameter is a placeholder. When you invoke the function, you are passing a value over to the parameter. This value will be referred to as the actual parameter or as the argument. The parameter list will then be able to refer to the number, order, and type of the parameters of the function. It is possible to work on a function that does not have any parameters at all.

- Function body: And finally, the function body is going to contain a collection of statements that are able to define what the function does.

There are a lot of times when we are going to be able to use the functions to help us get some parts of our code done and to ensure that we get it all set up and ready to handle. Make sure to practice these functions to see how they are going to work for our needs.

The Types of Modifiers

Any time that you are working with some of the codes that you want to do in C++, you will find that you will be able to use char, double, and int in order to allow the modifier that shows up before it to be there. The modifier that we are talking about here is going to be used to help us alter up the meaning of that base type so that it is going to fit into any program or situation that we are trying to create. There are going to be different types of modifiers of the data that we are able to work with. These include signed, unsigned, long, and short.

These four modifiers are going to be applicable to any of the base types of integers that we have. You are able to take the signed and unsigned, for example, in order to work with a char, and then long can be used on a double for example. C++ is also going to make it easier for us to work with shorthand notation to help with these integers. This means that they are able to use those words without needing to add in the "int" part since this is always implied in the coding.

There are also different types of qualifiers in order to get things to work on your C++ code. The following types of qualifiers that you will be able to use in order to provide some additional information about the variables the precede include:

- Const: Objects that have the "const" will not have the ability to be changed by the program while you are executing it.

- Volatile: The modifier of volatility will tell the compiler that you are able to change the value but these changes may not be explicitly specified by the program.

Restrict: a pointer that has been qualified by restricting is initially the only means by which an object it points to can be accessed.

CHAPTER - 2

BASIC FACILITIES

Array

The Array is a data structure that holds a sequential collection of elements of the same data type.

For example, in the code below I declared two arrays of different data type: an array of characters and an array of integers.

```cpp
#include <iostream>
int main(int argc, char* argv[])
{
    int i;
    int length;
    int sum = 0;
    char char_array[10] = { 'p', 's', 'y', 'c', 'h', 'o', 'l', 'o', 'g', 'y' };
    // total number of bytes allocated for that array
```

```cpp
    //one char is one byte: the number of elements =
number of bytes

    length = sizeof(char_array);

    std::cout << "Size of array of characters is " << length <<
std::endl;

    for (i = 0; i<length; i++)

    std::cout << char_array[i];

    std::cout << '\n';

    std::cout << '\n';

    std::cout << '\n';

    int numbers[10] = { 1, 5, 9, 4, 2, 7, 6, 3, 8, 0 };

    //the total number of bytes allocated for that array.

    length = sizeof(numbers);

    std::cout << "Size of numbers array=" << length <<
std::endl;

    //the total number of bytes allocated for array/number
of bytes allocated for one element

    length = sizeof(numbers) / sizeof(numbers[0]);

     std::cout << "Numbers of elements=" << length <<
std::endl;

      for (i = 0; i<length; i++)

      {

        sum = sum + numbers[i];

          std::cout << "Sum of numbers=" << sum <<
std::endl;

      }
```

```cpp
    int *p = numbers;

        std::cout << "Address of the first element is " << p <<
std::endl;

        std::cout << "The value in the address is " << *p <<
std::endl;

        p++; //move pointer to the next element

        std::cout << "Address of the second element is " <<
p << std::endl;

        std::cout << "The value in the address is " << *p <<
std::endl;

        int hold = 1;

        std::cin >> hold;

    return 0;

}
```

The function sizeof returns the number of bytes allocated for the array. Since char data type occupies one byte, the number of bytes returned by the sizeof function equals to the number of elements of the char array.

The integer data type occupies 4 bytes in the memory, and an array of 10 integers is stored in 40 bytes. As a result, the sizeof the array function returns 40 bytes for the integer array of 10 elements.

To calculate how many elements are stored in an array we can divide the number of bytes allocated for the whole array by the number of bytes allocated to one element of the array;

length=sizeof(numbers) / sizeof(numbers[0]);

40 / 4 = 10

To access the value of a single element, we have to use the array index. The index of array in C++ starts from 0.

The index of the first element is 0, the index of the second element is 1, and so on.

To access all elements of an array, we have to use for loop.

```
for(i=0; i<length; i++)

cout<<char_array[i];
```

If we declare a pointer and assign the array to the pointer, the pointer will hold the address of the first element of the array:

```
int *p =numbers;

cout<<"Address of the first element is "<<p<<endl;
```

The output of that line of code is:

Address of the first element is 0059F710

To access the value stored in the address of the first element of the array using the pointer, run the following line of code:

```
cout<<"The value in the address is "<<*p<<endl;
```

The output of the code is:

The value in the address is 1.

To move to the next element of the array, you have to increase p-value.

p++;

Now it will point to the second element of the array:

cout<<"Address of the second element is "<<p<<endl;

cout<<"The value in the address is"<<*p<<endl;

The output is:

The address of the second element of the numbers array on my PC is 0059F714

The value in the address of the second element is 5.

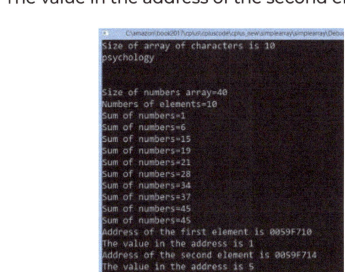

Figure The array program output.

String

String functions

I will show you how to use some of the string functions.

strcpy_s () - copies the content of a string to another.

strcat_s() - appends a copy of the source string to the destination string.

strlen() - returns the length of a string.

Our application will read the string from user input, copy it to another string, then copy the original string characters in the reverse sequence to the temporary string and concatenate the copy and the reversed copy in one string.

For example, if user enters string 'Concatenation' then the application will output

'ConcatenationnoitanetacnoC'

The following header files must be included in the main.cpp file:

#include "stdafx.h"

#include <stdio.h>

#include <cctype>

#include <iostream>

#include <cstring>

The <cstring> header is needed for the string functions: strcpy_s(), strcat_s() and strlen(). The cctype header file is needed for the toupper() function.

I want to explain how I copied characters from the original string to a temporary string in reversed order.

First, I got the length of the original string, using the strlen() function.

length=strlen(aWord);

Then in the loop, I copied the last character of the original string to the first place of the temporary string and so on.

Let us examine the code in the loop.

for(i=0; i <length; i++)

temp[i]=aWord[length-(i+1)];

If an user enters the word 'Concatenation' then the word length will be 13. The index of the first character in a string is 0, then the index of the last character of the string will be 12. It means that the index of the last character is length -1.

A line of code that I placed in the loop is

temp[i]=aWord[length-(i+1)];

When i =0, temp[i] will refer to the first character of the temp string.

At the same time (when i =0) the aWord [length-(i+1)] will refer to the aWord[13 – (0 + 1)] character and it will be aWord[12] that is the last character of the 'Concatenation' string.

When i=1, the temp [1] will refer to the second character of the temp string and aWord [13-(1+1)] will refer to the second from the end character of the 'Concatenation' string.

That way, we can copy all characters in reversed order.

When we have copied all the characters from the original string to the temp string, we need to add null to the end of the temp string, because a string in C++ must be terminated with null.

The line of code temp[length]='\0'; will do the job.

The whole code is included in visual_studio_2017. zip.

```
#include "stdafx.h" #include <stdio.h>

#include <cctype>

#include <cstring>

#include <iostream>

int main()
```

```cpp
{
    char more = 'Y';
    char prompt1[] = "\nEnter a word not more than 20 characters and press enter.\n";
    char prompt3[] = "\nDo you want to continue? Y/N\n";
    char aWord[20];
    char aCopy[40];
    int length = 0;
    char temp[20];
    int i;
        while (toupper(more) == 'Y')
        {
        std::cout << prompt1;
        std::cin >> aWord;
        std::cout << "aWord=" << aWord << std::endl;
        strcpy_s(aCopy, aWord);
        std::cout << "aCopy=" << aCopy <<
        std::endl; length = strlen(aWord);
        std::cout << "length=" << length <<
        std::endl;
            //fill temp[] array with the word characters in opposite order.
            for (i = 0; i < length; i++)
            temp[i] = aWord[length - (i + 1)];
            temp[length] = '\0';
```

```cpp
        std::cout << "Temp=" << temp <<std::endl;

        strcat_s(aCopy, temp);

        std::cout << "aCopy after concatenation of
temp=" << aCopy << std::endl;

        std::cout << prompt3;

        std::cin >> more;

    }

  return 0;

}
```

Output:

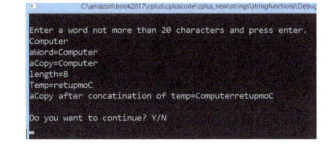

Figure String manipulation.

Lists

Let us imagine a puzzle. You have a row of boxes. Each box contains a card with one letter. You have to figure out the sequence of the letters, so that the letters compose a word.

T	C	O	N	E	L	Y	G	O	H
5	10	6	3	2	9	1	7	8	4

Figure A linked list

In the table above, you can see that each box has a number. You may guess that these numbers are the key to the puzzle. The first box has a letter T inside and number 5 on the front side. Take a card with the letter T and put it aside. The number 5 may point to the next letter. Count boxes. The fifth box has the letter 'E.' Take the card with the 'E' letter and place it next to T. You will get "TE." The box with the letter 'E' has number 2 on its side. So, take the card from the 2nd box and place it next to "TE." You will get "TEC."

The box with the letter 'C' has the number 10, so take the card from the 10th box. You will get "TECH." The box with the letter 'H' has number 4, so take the card from the 4th box. You got "TECHN." Continue following the numbers, and you will get the whole word: TECHNOLOGY.

That is how a linked list works. It is made of nodes. Each node has at least one variable that holds data (a text or number or object) and one variable (pointer) that holds the address of the next node. This system walks through the node list as you did in the puzzle. The pointer of the last node has null value, or it may point to the first node. Then we have a closed linked list.

ADD A NODE

If you want to add a new node to the end of the

linked list, you have to create a new node. Then point the pointer of the last node to the address of the new node and assign null to the new node pointer.

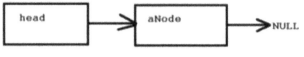

Figure Adding a node to the end of the linked list.

If you want to add a new node to the beginning of the linked list, you have to create a new node. Point the pointer of the new node to the first node, and that is it.

Figure Adding a node to the head of the linked list.

If you need to add a node in the middle of the linked list, you have to create a new node, and then break the chain: redirect the node (previous to the break), to a new node and point the pointer of the new node to the next node (the one after the break).

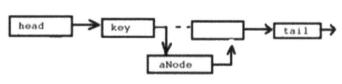

Figure Adding a node in the middle of the linked list.

DELETE A NODE

To delete a node with a certain key, you walk along with the list until you find the key. Then you assign the key node to the temp node. Then you point the node previous to the key node to the node next to the key node. See Figure 60. As a result, the temp key becomes isolated from the list. Now you can delete the temp.

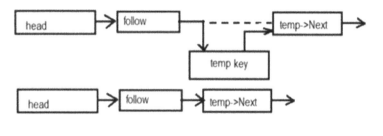

Figure Delete a node.

Below is a code for Node class. For simplicity sake, I created a node that holds an integer and node pointer to the next node. Both class member variables are declared as private. It is good programming practice not to use global variables, because private members cannot be seen from the outside of the class. We still need to set and to read these private member variables. The public functions set and will do the job.

CHAPTER - 3
BINARY TREES

Binary trees are one of the most useful of all the basic data structures and are by far the most interesting. They are the perfect example of how recursion and pointers can be used to do some very useful things.

One of the best techniques for creating lists of things is the linked list, but finding an element in the list can take a while. And, if you have a large amount of unstructured data, an array won't help much either. You can try sorting the array but, even so, inserting items into it will still be difficult. If you have an array that you want to keep sorted, inserting new elements will take a lot of shuffling! And trying to find things in a list as quickly as possible is quite important, especially in scenarios like these:

- You're building an MMORPG game and players need to be able to sign in quickly—that involves quickly looking players up

- You're building software to process credit cards and millions of transactions need to be handled hourly—credit card balances need to found very quickly

- You're using a low-power device, such as a tablet or smartphone, and showing your users an address book. You don't want your users to keep hanging because your data structure is slow.

This section will discuss the tools needed to overcome these problems and more.

The idea of the solution is to be able to store elements in a structure like a linked list, using pointers to help structure the memory, but in an easier way than the linked list. Doing this requires that the memory have more structure than a simple list.

So what does structuring data mean? When we started this journey, we only had arrays, but these never really gave us the ability to use data structures other than sequential lists. Linked lists use pointers to grow sequential lists incrementally but don't use the flexibility of the pointer to build more sophisticated structures.

What are these more sophisticated structures in memory? Structures that hold more than a single next node at any given time are a good example. But why would you want this? Simple. If you have two "next nodes," one can be used to represent elements that are more than the current element. This is called a binary tree.

These are named because there are always one or two branches from every node. Each of the next nodes is a child, and the node that links to the child is the parent node.

This is what a binary tree might look like:

10

6 14

5 8 11 18

In the tree, the left child on each of the elements is smaller than the element, and the right child is larger. 10 is the parent node for the whole tree, and the child nodes of 6 and 14 are both parent nodes to their own small trees, called subtrees.

Binary trees have one very important property: each child is an entire tree. Combine this with the rule of the left child being smaller and the right child being larger, and you have an easy way of defining algorithms that locate specific nodes in the tree.

First, look at the current node value. If it equals the search target, it's done. If it's more than the search target, go left; otherwise, go right. This works because each node to the left of the tree is less than the current mode value, and each on the right is more.

In an ideal world, your binary tree will be balanced with the exact same number of nodes on both sides. In such cases, every child tree is roughly 50 percent of the entire tree and, when you search the tree for a value, the search can eliminate 50 percent of the results each time it gets to a child node. So, if you had a tree of 1000 elements, 500 would be immediately eliminated. Search that tree again (it only has 50 elements now), and you can cut it by about 50 percent again. That way it doesn't take long to find the value you want.

So, how many times must a tree be subdivided before you get to one element? The answer to that is log2n (n is the number of elements the tree has). This is a small value, even if your tree is large—if your tree had, say, 32 billion elements, the value would be 32; almost 100 million times faster than a search of a linked list of four billion elements, where every single one has to be assessed.

If the tree isn't balanced, you won't be able to eliminate roughly half of the elements; worst case, each node only has one child and that makes the tree nothing more than a linked list with a few extra pointers, thus requiring you to search all elements.

So, when a tree is balanced approximately, it's much faster and easier to search for nodes than the same search on a linked list. This is because you can structure the memory of how you want it.

Implementing a Binary Tree

To implement a binary tree, begin by declaring the node structure:

Struct node

```
{
int key_value;

node *p_left;

node *p_right;

};
```

The node can store values as a simple integer, key_value, and has two child trees —p_left, and p_right.

There are some common functions that you want on your binary tree: inserting, searching, removing, and destroying:

node* insert (node* p_tree, int key);

node *search (node* p_tree, int key);

void destroyTree (node* p_tree);

node *remove (node* p_tree, int key);

Inserting

We'll use a recursive algorithm for inserting it into the tree. Recursion is fantastic for trees because there are two small trees for each tree; that makes the entire tree recursive by nature. The function takes a key and a tree that already exists (even an empty one) and returns a new tree that has the inserted value.

node* insert (node *p_tree, int key)

```
{
// base case--we have got to an empty tree and our new node
// needs to be inserted here
if ( p_tree == NULL )
{
node* p_new_tree = new node;
p_new_tree->p_left = NULL;
p_new_tree->p_right = NULL;
p_new_tree->key_value = key;
return p_new_tree;
}
// decide – left subtree or right subtree for the insertion
// depending on the what the node value is
if( key < p_tree->key_value )
{
// build a new tree from p_tree->left, and add in the key
// replace existing p_tree->left pointer with a pointer
// to new tree. Set the p_tree->p_left pointer
// in case p_tree->left is NULL. (If it isn't NULL,,
```

```
// p_tree->p_left won't change but it set it just
// to make sure.)
p_tree->p_left = insert( p_tree->p_left, key );
}
else
{
// Insertion into the right side is symmetric to the
// insertion in the left
p_tree->p_right = insert( p_tree->p_right, key );
}
return p_tree;
}
```

The basic logic here is this: if you have an empty tree, you create a new one. If not, the value for insertion goes to the left subtree if it's more than the current node, and the left subtree is then replaced with the new one. Otherwise, insert it into the right subtree and replace it.

When it comes to seeing it in action, build an empty tree into a tree with a couple of nodes. If the value 10 is inserted in the empty tree (NULL), immediately we will hit base case, and the result will be a tree of:

1

And both of the child trees will point to NULL.

Then insert 5 into the tree and make the following call:

insert(a tree with a parent , 5)

Because 5 is lower than 10, the call onto the left-subtree is recursive:

insert(NULL, 5)

insert(a tree with a parent , 5)

The call of

insert(NULL, 5)

creates and returns a new tree

5

When the returned tree is received, insert(,5) links the trees. In this example, 10's left child was NULL before. Therefore, the left child of 10 is established a new tree:

1

5

If we now add 7, we get:

insert(NULL, 7)

insert(a tree with a parent, 7)

insert(a tree with a parent , 7)

So, first off,

insert(NULL, 7)

will return a new tree:

7

And then

insert(a tree with a parent, 7)

will link to the subtree of 7 in this way:

5

7

Lastly, the tree gets returned to:

insert(a tree with a parent , 7)

And this will link it back:

10

5

7

Because there was already a pointer from 10 to the node with 5, it isn't really necessary to relink 10's left child to the tree with 5 as the parent, but it does eliminate one conditional check to see if the subtree is empty.

Destroying

This should also be a recursive function. Before deleting the current node, the algorithm destroys both of the subtrees that are at the current node.

void destroy_tree (node *p_tree)

```
{
if ( p_tree != NULL )
{
destroy_tree( p_tree->p_left );
destroy_tree( p_tree->p_right );
delete p_tree;
}
}
```

As a way of better understanding this, let's say that the value of the node was printed before the node was deleted:

void destroy_tree (node *p_tree)

```
{
if ( p_tree != NULL )
{
destroy_tree( p_tree->p_left );
destroy_tree( p_tree->p_right );
cout << "Deleting node: " << p_tree->key_value;
delete p_tree;
}
}
```

As you can see, the tree is deleted from the bottom

up. Nodes 5 and 8 go first, then 6, before moving to the other side and deleting 11 and 18, followed by 14. Lastly, 10 will be deleted. The tree values aren't important; what matters is where the node is. In the following binary tree, rather than the node values, we use the order of deletion:

7

3 6

1 2 4 5

It can be helpful to walk through the code manually on a few trees, so you can see it much clearer.

Deleting from trees is a great example of a recursive algorithm that's not easy to do as an iterative implementation. First, you need a loop that can deal with both sides of the tree at the same time. You need to be able to delete a subtree while simultaneously tracking the next one, and that needs to be done for every level. With the stack, you can keep your place much more easily. The best way of visualizing this is to say that each stack frame will store the tree branch that has been deleted or destroyed already:

destroy_tree( )

destroy_tree( )—knows whether the subtree was the left or right

Each of the stack frames knows which bits of the tree have to be destroyed because it knows what point in the function execution should continue. When the first call to destroy the tree is made, the program is notified by the stack frame to continue executing when the second call is made to destroy_tree. When that second call is made, the program is told to continue with the delete tree. Because every function has a stack frame of its own, it can track the entire state of the tree's destruction at the current time, one tree level at a time.

To implement this in a non-recursive way would require having a data structure that retains the same amount and type of information. You could, for example, write a function that holds a linked list as a way of simulating the list. That linked list would have subtrees that were being destroyed and trees left for destruction. Then a loop-based algorithm could be written to add the subtrees to the list and remove them after they were destroyed fully. Basically, recursion lets you use the stack data structure built-in rather than needing to write your own.

CHAPTER - 4
INHERITANCE

Example:

```cpp
#include <iostream>
using namespace std;
// defining a simple student class with 2 members
class Student
{
public:
    int studentID;
    string studentName;
// Function to display the members of the class
    void Display()
    {
        cout<<"Student ID "<<studentID<<endl;
        cout<<"Student Name "<<studentName;
    }
```

```
};
int main () {
Student stud1;
//Assigning values to the properties of the class
    stud1.studentID=1;
    stud1.studentName="John";
    stud1.Display();

    return 0;
}
```

With the above program:

- We have a class called 'Student' which has 2 members, one is 'studentID' and the other is called 'studentName'.

- We then define a member function called 'Display()' which outputs the 'studentID' and 'studentName' to the console.

- We can then call the member function from the object in the main program.

With this program, the output is as follows:

Student ID 1

Student Name John

So Then What is Inheritance?

Inheritance is a concept wherein we can define

a class to inherit the properties and methods of another class. This helps in not having the need to define the class again or having the properties and methods defined again.

Let's say that we had a class called 'Person,' which had a property of 'Name' and a method of 'Display.' Then through inheritance, we can define a class called Student, which could inherit the Person class. The Student class would automatically get the ID member and the Display function. The Student class could then define its own additional members if required.

To define an inherited class, we use the following syntax.

Derived class:Base class

Here the 'Derived class' is the class that will inherit the properties of the other class, known as the 'Base class.'

So if we had a base class with a property and a function as shown below.

Base class

```
{
Public or protected:
Property1;
}
```

Then when we define the derived class from the base class, the derived class will have access to the property. Note that the property and function need to have the access modifier as public or protected. We will look at access modifiers in greater detail later on.

Derived class: Base Class

```
{

// No need to define property1, it will automatically
inherit these.

}
```

Now let's look at a simple example of inheritance via code.

Example 2: The following program is used to showcase how to use a simple inherited class.

```
#include <iostream>

using namespace std;

// Defining  a simple Person class with a property of Name

class Person
{
public:
    string Name;
};
```

// Here we have the derived class. It defines another property of ID

class Student: public Person

```cpp
{
public:
    int ID;
// Function to display both ID and Name. Since Name is available from the base class of Person, we are able to access it here.
 void Display()
    {
        cout<<"Student ID "<<ID<<endl;
        cout<<"Student Name "<<Name;
    }
};
int main () {
Student stud1;
    stud1.ID=1;
    stud1.Name="John";
    stud1.Display();
    return 0;
}
```

With the above program:

- We are defining a class called 'Person' that has one member called 'Name.'

- We then use inheritance to define the 'Student' class. Notice that we now define another property called 'ID.'

- In the 'Display' function, note that we can use the 'Name' property without the need for defining it in the 'Student' class again.

With this program, the output is as follows:

Student ID 1

Student Name John

Now we have seen how to use derived and base classes, which is also known as inheritance.

1.2 Functions in Derived Classes

We can also define functions that can be inherited from base classes. Let's see how we can achieve this.

If we, for instance, had a base class with a property and a function as shown below.

Base class

```
{
Public or protected:
Property1;
Fucntion1;
}
```

When we define the derived class from the base class, the derived class will have access to the property and the function as well. Note that the property and function need to have the access modifier as either public or protected.

Derived class: Base Class

```
{
// No need to define property1 and Function1, it will automatically inherit these.

}
```

Let's now look at an example where we can use functions in derived classes.

Example 3: The following program is used to showcase how to use an inherited class with functions.

```cpp
#include <iostream>

using namespace std;

// Defining a simple Person class with a property of Name, ID, and also a function called Display.

class Person

{
public:

    string Name;

    int ID;

    void Display()

    {

        cout<<"ID "<<ID<<endl;
```

```cpp
        cout<<"Name "<<Name;
    }
};
// The Student class simply derives itself from the
Person base class
class Student:public Person {
};
int main () {
// Since the derived class has access to the properties
and functions of the base class , these can be accessed
via the Student object
Student stud1;
    stud1.ID=1;
    stud1.Name="John";
    stud1.Display();
    return 0;
}
```

With this program, the output is as follows:

ID 1

Name John

We can also redefine the Display function in the Student class. But if you look at the above example, you will notice that the Display function in the Person class has the display text as ID and Name. But suppose we wanted to have the display name as Student ID and Student name in the student class, we can redefine the Display function. Let's look at an example of this.

Example 4: The following program shows how to use an inherited class with redefined functions.

```cpp
#include <iostream>

using namespace std;

class Person
{
public:
    string Name;
    int ID;
    void Display()
    {
        cout<<"ID "<<ID<<endl;
        cout<<"Name "<<Name;
    }
};
class Student:public Person {
public:
// Here we are redefining the Display function
    void Display()
    {
        cout<<"Student ID "<<ID<<endl;
```

```
        cout<<"Student Name "<<Name;
    }
};
int main () {
Student stud1;
    stud1.ID=1;
    stud1.Name="John";
    stud1.Display();
    return 0;
}
```

With this program, the output is as follows:

Student ID 1

Student Name John

1.3 Multiple Inheritance

We can also make the derived class inherit from multiple base classes. This helps in getting more functionality out of multiple classes all at once.

Derived class: base class1, base class2... base classN

Here you just need to separate the base classes with a comma.

So if we had a base class with a property and a function as shown below.

Base class1

```
{
Public or protected:
Property1;
Fuction1;
}
```

And another base class as follows.

Base class2

```
{
Public or protected:
Property2;
Fucntion2;
}
```

Then when we define the derived class from both of the base classes, the derived class will have access to the property and the function of both classes.

Derived class: Base Class1, Base Class2

```
{

// No need to define property1, property2, and
Function1, Fucntion2 it will automatically inherit these.

}
```

Again note that the property and function need

to have the access modifier as either public or protected. Let's look at an example of multiple derived classes.

Example 5: The following program is used to showcase how to use multiple derived classes.

```cpp
#include <iostream>
using namespace std;
// Defining the first base class of Person
class Person
{
public:
    string Name;
    int ID;
    void Display()
    {
        cout<<"ID"<<ID<<endl;
        cout<<"Name"<<Name;
    }
};
// Defining the second base class of Marks
class Marks
{
public:
    int marks1,marks2;
    void Sum()
    {
```

```cpp
          cout<<marks1+marks2;
   }
};
// The derived class inherits from both the Person and
Marks base class.
class Student:public Person,public Marks {
public:
   void Display()
   {
      cout<<"Student ID "<<ID<<endl;
      cout<<"Student Name "<<Name<<endl;
   }
};
int main () {
Student stud1;
   stud1.ID=1;
   stud1.Name="John";
   stud1.Display();
   stud1.marks1=5;
   stud1.marks2=10;
   stud1.Sum();
   return 0;
}
```

With the above program:

- We are defining 2 base classes, one is called

'Person', and the other is called 'Marks.'

- The derived class 'Student' derives both classes and is able to use the members from both classes.

With this program, the output is as follows:

Student ID 1

Student Name John

15

1.4 Access Control

Class modifiers can be used to define the visibility of properties and methods in a class. Below are the various modifiers available.

- Private—With private, the properties and methods are only available to the class itself.

- Protected—With protected, the properties and methods are only available to the class itself and subclasses derived from that class.

- Public—With public, the properties and methods are available to all classes.

Let's say we had the following structure for a class.

Class classname

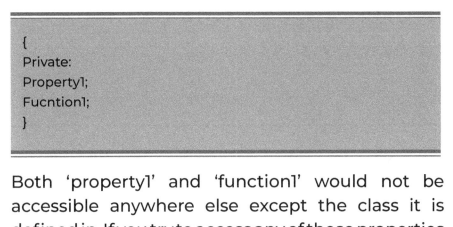

```
{
Private:
Property1;
Fucntion1;
}
```

Both 'property1' and 'function1' would not be accessible anywhere else except the class it is defined in. If you try to access any of these properties or functions from the main program, you will get a compile-time error.

Now let's define the class below, but this time we'll use the protected access modifier.

Class classname1

```
{
Protected:
Property1;
Fucntion1;
}
```

Now 'property1' and 'function1' are accessible from both the above class and any other class that derives from it.

So if we had the below-derived class definition, we would be able to access both 'property1' and 'fucntion1' in the derived class. But note that we will not be able to use these properties in any other non-derived class.

Class derivedclassname: classname1

```
{
}
```

Let' look at another example of access modifiers.

Example 6: The following program is used to showcase how to use access modifiers.

#include <iostream>

using namespace std;

class Person

```
{
public:
    int ID;
protected:
// Note that we are defining the Name property as protected
    string Name;
    void Display()
    {
        cout<<"ID "<<ID<<endl;
        cout<<"Name "<<Name;
    }
// Note that we have defined the city property as private
private:
    string city;
};
class Student:public Person {
public:
    void Display()
```

```
    {
        cout<<"Student ID "<<ID<<endl;
        cout<<"Student Name "<<Name<<endl;
    }
};
int main () {
Student stud1;
    stud1.ID=1;
    stud1.Name="John";
    stud1.Display();
    return 0;
}
```

With this program, the output is as follows:

error:'std::__cxx11::string Person::Name' is protected

Why are we getting this error? The 'person' class has 2 properties called ID and Name. The name has the protected access modifier, which means that it can only be accessed in the derived class. But we are trying to access it in the main class, which is wrong. Hence the correct way to implement this is as follows.

Example 7: The following program shows how to use access modifiers in the proper way.

#include <iostream>

using namespace std;

class Person

```cpp
{
public:
    int ID;
protected:
    string Name;
    void Display()
    {
        cout<<"ID "<<ID<<endl;
        cout<<"Name "<<Name;
    }
private:
    string city;
};
class Student:public Person {
public:
// We have now defined a function which can set the value of
the protected property accordingly.
    void InputName(string pName)
    {
        Name=pName;
    }
    void Display()
    {
        cout<<"Student ID "<<ID<<endl;
        cout<<"Student Name "<<Name<<endl;
    }
};
int main () {
```

```
Student stud1;
    stud1.ID=1;
    stud1.InputName("John");
    stud1.Display();
    return 0;
}
```

In the above program, we now correctly define a method called 'InputName' in the 'Student' class, which can access the protected 'Name' member.

With this program, the output is as follows:

Student ID 1

Student Name John

Now let's look at the same example and try to display the property called 'City,' which is defined in the 'Person' class.

Example 8: The following program shows a second example of how to use access modifiers the wrong way.

```
#include <iostream>

using namespace std;

class Person
```

```cpp
{
public:
    int ID;
protected:
    string Name;
    void Display()
    {
        cout<<"ID "<<ID<<endl;
        cout<<"Name "<<Name;
    }
private:
    string city;
};
class Student:public Person {
public:
    void InputName(string pName)
    {
        Name=pName;
    }
    void Display()
    {
        cout<<"Student ID "<<ID<<endl;
// Note that we are trying to use the private property in the
derived class.
        cout<<"Student city "<<city<<endl;
        cout<<"Student Name "<<Name<<endl;
    }
};
```

```
int main () {
Student stud1;
    stud1.ID=1;
    stud1.InputName("John");
    stud1.Display();
    return 0;
}
```

With this program, the output is as follows:

error: 'std::__cxx11::string Person::city' is private

Since the 'City' property is private, it cannot even be used in the derived class. We can only work with this property in the 'Person' class.

CHAPTER - 5

ADVANCED BASIC

Pointers

Pointers have been mentioned previously, and they are the memory address of a variable, this is much like a house address for a person. These can be passed around a parameter and allow the effects of passing by reference mentioned previously.

The program below will show the address of a variable:

```c
#include <stdio.h>
int main()
{
int var;
printf("The address is: %x\n", &var);
return 0;
}
```

Output:

> The address is: 10ffa2c

Note: This will be different almost every time you run

Note the highlighted statement, the '&' (Reference Operator) is used to return the memory location of the variable and allows certain statements to access the data in that location. The '%x' is used because a memory location is in hexadecimal.

To create a pointer, we use the dereferencing operator (*), this will create a pointer variable that is designed to hold a memory locations address. Below is a program that creates a pointer and uses reference operator (&) to store another regular variable's address in the newly created pointer. The dereferencing operator (*) is also used to access or change the actual data in that memory location.

- Dereferencing operator (*) is used to create a pointer, it is also used when changing the actual value

- Referencing operator (&) is used when obtaining the memory location of a pointer

//Regular variable

int var = 10;

//Pointer

int* pointer;

```
//Storing of var memory location
pointer = &var;
//Pointer is now effecivly 'var' so
//things like this can happen
*pointer = 20;
printf("Var's value is now: %d", var);
```

Output:

>Var's value is now: 20

NULL pointers

When you create a pointer, is it initially not given anything to point at, this is dangerous because the pointer when created it references random memory, and changing this data in the memory location can crash the program. To prevent this, when we create a pointer we assign it to NULL like so:

```
int* pointer = NULL;
```

This means the pointer has an address of '0', this is a reserved memory location to identify a null pointer. A null pointer can be checked by an if statement:

```
if (pointer){}
```

This will succeed if the pointer isn't null.

Using pointers

Now some real-world uses of pointers are passing

them as parameters and effectively passing them by reference. The example below will show the effect:

void Change_Value(int* reference)

```
{
//Changes the value in the memory location
*reference = 20;
}
int main()
{
//Creates pointer to variable
int var = 10;
int* pointer = &var;
printf("The value before call: %d\n", var);
//Method call
Change_Value(pointer);
//Prints new value
printf("The value after call: %d\n", var);
return 0;
}
```

Output:

>The value before call: 10

>The value after call: 20

This passes the memory location, not the value of the variable, meaning you have the location where you can make changes.

Note the parameter is int* this is the pointer type, so for an example of a pointer to a char would be char*.

Pointer Arithmetic

There are times when moving a pointer along to another memory location might be useful; this is where pointer arithmetic comes into use. If we were to execute say ptr++ and the ptr was an integer pointer it would now move 4bytes (Size of an int) along, and we were to run it again, another 4bytes etc. This can mean pointer (if pointing to valid array structures) can act much like an array can. An example is below:

int arrayInt[] = { 10, 20, 30 };

size_t arrayInt_Size = 3;

//Will point to the first array index

int* ptr = &arrayInt;

for (int i = 0; i < arrayInt_Size; i++)

```
{
//Remember, *ptr gets the value in the memory location
printf("Value of arrayInt[%d] = %d\n", i, *ptr);
ptr++;
}
```

Output:

>Value of arrayInt[0] = 10

>Value of arrayInt[1] = 20

>Value of arrayInt[2] = 30

This shows that a pointer to the first address of the array can be incremented along the addresses of the array (Remember each value of an array is stored in neighbouring memory locations)

You can do the opposite and decrement a pointer i.e. make the pointers value decrease.

There is also way to compare pointers using relational operators such as ==, < and >. The most common use for this is checking if two pointer point to the same location:

```
int value;

//Assigns ptr1 and prt2 the same value

int* ptr1 = &value;

int* ptr2 = &value;

//ptr3 is assigned another value

int* ptr3 = NULL;

if (ptr1 == ptr2)
```

```
{
printf("ptr1 and ptr2 are equal!\n");
}
if (!ptr1 == ptr3)
{
printf("ptr1 is not equal to ptr3\n");
}
```

This checks if the various pointers are equal. The same can be done with > and <.

Function pointers

Much like you can do with variables, you can also do the same with functions; below is a snippet of code that shows a function pointer being defined. Key sections will be highlighted:

void printAddition(int value1, int value2)

```
{
int result = value1 + value2;
printf("The result is: %d", result);
}
int main()
{
//Function pointer definition
//<retrunType>(*<Name>)(<Parameters>)
void(*functionPtr)(int, int);
```

```
functionPtr = &printAddition;
//Invoking call to pointer function
(*functionPtr)(100, 200);
return 0;
}
```

The basic structure for defining a function pointer is like so

<Return_Type> (*<Name>) (<Parameters>)

Where in this case:

<Return_Type> = void

<Name> = functionPtr

<Parameters> = int, int

This function pointer can now be passed as a parameter and used in situations where you would want to change the behaviour of code but with almost the same code.

An example could be dynamically choosing what operation a calculator should perform (Note: this is complex code and should be used a rough example, so don't worry if you don't fully understand)

void calculator(int value1, int value2, int(*opp)(int,int))

```c
{
int result = (*opp)(value1, value2);
printf("The result from the operation: %d\n", result);
}
//Adds two values
int add(int num1, int num2)
{
return num1 + num2;
}
//Subtracts two values
int sub(int num1, int num2)
{
return num1 - num2;
}
int main()
{
calculator(10, 20, &add);
calculator(10, 20, &sub);
return 0;
}
```

Here what is happening we are passing the function 'add' and 'sub' as parameters for the function calculator, as you see from the highlight the function parameter is defined like it is above with the return type, name and parameters being defined, all that is passed into calculator is &add and &sub for the function pointers. The calculator function then goes on to invoke the pointer and passes in the values and returns the result.

Storage Classifications

In C each variable can be given a storage class that can define certain characteristics.

The classes are:

- Automatic variables
- Static variables
- Register variables
- External variables

Automatic variables

Every variable we have defined so far has been an automatic variable; they are created when a function is called and automatically destroyed when a function exits. These variables are also known as local variables.

auto int value;

Is the same as

int value;

Static variables

Static is used when you want to keep the variable from being destroyed when it goes out of scope; this variable will persist until the program is complete. The static variable is created only once throughout the lifetime of the program. Below is an example of a static variable in use:

```c
void tick()
{
//This will run once
static int count = 0;
count++;
printf("The count is now: %d\n", count);
}
int main()
{
tick();
tick();
tick();
}
```

Output:

>The count is now: 1

>The count is now: 2

>The count is now: 3

The area highlighted section is the static definition and will only run once.

Register variables

The register is used to define a variable that is to be store in register memory opposed to regular memory, the benefits register memory has is it is much much quicker to access; however, there is only space for a few variables.

Defining a register variable is done like so:

register int value;

External variable

We touched on this before, but a global variable is a variable not defined in a scope and, therefore, can be used anywhere. An external variable Is a variable defined in a separate location like another file, and the extern keyword is used to signify that the variable is in another file. You would include another file as a reference by placing this at the top of your file:

#include "FileName.c"

This is to tell the program to reference this file as well. Note the files need to be in the same location.

Program 1 [File_2.c]

#include <stdio.h>

#include "C_TUT.c"

```c
int main()
{
extern int globalValue;
printf("The global variable is: %d", globalValue);

}
```

Program 2 (It is small) [C_TUT.c]

#include <stdio.h>

int globalValue = 1032;

The Output of running File_2.c:

>The global variable is: 1032

This shows that the globalValue is referenced from C_TUT.c and used in another file by using the extern keyword.

We touched on recursion in the basic section of the tutorial, and again it's the definition of a function´s tasks with definition to itself. As promised, there are a few more examples of recursion explained below:

```c
int factorial(int x)
{
int r;
//Stopping condition
if (x == 1)
{
//Has a conclusion so looping stop
return 1;
}
else
{
//Recursive definition
return r = x * factorial(x - 1);
}
```

```
}
int main()
{
puts("Please enter a number: ");
//Reads in user input
int a, b;
scanf("%d", &a);
//Starts the execution
b = factorial(a);
printf("The factorial is: %d", b);

}
```

This is the world-famous example of recursion that is used to find a factorial of a number (3 factorial is 3x2x1). It works by the recursive return statement above; it stops by having a return statement without a recursive definition, i.e. when x = 1, the function just returns 1; this means the stack can unwind and find an answer. There is a flow diagram below:

Recursion

Recursion is a difficult concept and will only be lightly touched on here, and its real-world uses and functionality explained in the advanced section.

Recursion is a definition of a functions commands involving a reference to itself, yes very confusing, I know, but I use some examples to explain.

const int maxLoops = 5;

void Sequence(int previous, int now, size_t loopCount)

```
{
//Works out next value
int next = previous + now;
//Prints new value
printf("New value: %d\n", next);
//Increments counts
loopCount++;
//Stopping condition to make sure infinite looping doesn't occur
if (loopCount < maxLoops)
{
//Recursive call
Sequence(now, next, loopCount);
}
}
int main()
{
Sequence(1, 1, 0);
}
```

Output:

>New value: 2

>New value: 3

>New value: 5

>New value: 8

>New value: 13

There're a few things to note, the lack of iteration loops, recursion in its essence causes looping. The second thing to note if the if statement labelled 'stopping condition,' if recursive set-ups don't have conditions that stop them looping they will loop forever, so this is a crucial element for using recursion effectively.

We touched on recursion in the basic section of the tutorial, and again it's the definition of a function´s tasks with definition to itself. As promised, there are a few more examples of recursion explained below:

```
int factorial(int x)
{
int r;
//Stopping condition
if (x == 1)
{
//Has a conclusion so looping stop
return 1;
}
else
{
//Recursive definition
return r = x * factorial(x - 1);
}
}
int main()
```

```
{
puts("Please enter a number: ");
//Reads in user input
int a, b;
scanf("%d", &a);
//Starts the execution
b = factorial(a);
printf("The factorial is: %d", b);
}
```

This is the world-famous example of recursion that is used to find a factorial of a number (3 factorial is 3x2x1). It works by the recursive return statement above; it stops by having a return statement without a recursive definition, i.e. when x = 1, the function just returns 1; this means the stack can unwind and find an answer. There is a flow diagram below:

```
function factorial(3) {
    if (3 === 0)
        return 1;
    else {
        return x * factorial(3 - 1);
    }
}

let num = 3;
let result = factorial(3);

function factorial(2) {
    if (2 === 0)
        return 1;
    else {
        return x * factorial(2 - 1);
    }
}

function factorial(1) {
    if (1 === 0)
        return 1;
    else {
        return x * factorial(1 - 1);
    }
}

function factorial(0) {
    if (3 === 0)
        return 1;
    else {
        return x * factorial(1 - 1);
    }
}
```

2* 3 = 6 is returned

1* 2 = 2 is returned

1* 1 = 1 is returned

1 is returned

2

1

0

CHAPTER - 6

STL CONTAINERS AND ITERATORS

Containers

ontainers are the primary contribution of the STL, and they are for holding and accessing a sequence of objects. The STL provides different types of containers, such as vector, list, map, and hash tables. However, based on the characteristics of data arrangement, the STL containers are categorized into three major sections:

1. Sequence containers such as vector, fixed-size array, list, forward_list, and deque;

2. Associative containers:

a. Ordered (sorted) associative containers such as set, multiset, map, and multimap;

b. Unordered (unsorted) associative containers such as unordered_set, unordered_multiset, unordered_map and unordered_multimap;

3. Container adapters such as stack, queue, and priority_queue.

In addition to these fully qualified containers, C++ provides three almost qualified containers, viz., string, built-in-array and valarray.

Each of the containers are sophisticated template classes with the default constructor, constructor from arguments, copy constructor, assignment operator, and definite destructor. Apart from that, most of the containers define its own iterator, and every container has its own operation member functions.

Container iterators

From those sections, we know that each container provides its own iterator and using that iterator operations are performed on the elements of the container.

Among the five categories of iterators, each container defines any one of the three categories, viz.,

Forward iterators:

- Can read;

- Can write;

- Can be repeated read/write at a single location;

- Can move forward (++), but cannot move backwards, thus the name forward iterator;

- Is used in: unordered associative containers and forward list, which are for the best space-efficient storage.

- Bidirectional iterator:

- Is same as the forward iterator, but it can also move backwards (so, ++ as well as --), thus is named bidirectional; and

- Is used in containers: list, set, map, multiset, and multimap.

- Random access iterator:

- Is the same as the bidirectional iterator, but it can jump (+=N or –=N, where N is a whole number) instead of (+=1 or -=1, where +=1 is ++ and -=1 is --), thus is named random access iterator(jump iterator); and

- Is used in containers: vector, string, deque and array<T,N>.

Apart from helping the operations of STL algorithms in the containers, the iterators also help in executing internal operations (member functions) of the containers.

Some internal operations are common to all the sequence and associative containers, and they are:

O(1):

begin(), end(),   cbegin(), cend(),   rbegin()*, rend()*, crbegin()*, crend()*,   empty(), swap(),   size()†, max_size(), shrink_to_fit()‡, emplace() and emplace_back()*;

O(n):

Assignment operator: =,

Relational operators:

!=, ==, <††, <=††, >†† and >=††, and clear();

O (variable):

- Insert()†, erase()† and emplace()†(they are fast in node-based containers and slow in (middle of) contiguous-memory containers); and

- Constructors (usually, the composition of classes or

- Their default constructors have constant complexity, but all other constructors and destructors may have linear complexity).

Note:

a) The forward list and unordered associative containers use forward iterators so they do not have the reverse iterator operations: emplace back(), rbegin(), rend), crbegin() and crend().

b) The associative containers support reverse iterators, but they do not support emplace back. This is so because the associative containers keep their elements in a sorted order, so it does not accept the command emplace back (), which insist on placing the new element at the back of the container.

†The forward list:

1. Does not support the operator size();

2. Instead of insert(), erase() and emplace(), it provides insert after(), erase after() and emplace after();

3. Has special iterators before begin(), cbefore begin(), such that

- an operation in forward list:

- my_fwd_list.insert_after

- (my_fwd_list.before_begin(), inv_data.gold);

- is equivalent to the following operation in list:

- my_list.insert

- (my_list.begin(), inv_data.gold);

- Note:

- None of the containers can write or read beyond end(), i.e.,

- my_fwd_list.insert_after

- (my_fwd_list.end(), inv_data.gold); is an error!

‡ shrink to fit () requests the removal of unused memory capacity and it is applicable only to vector, deque and string.

†† The unorder containers do not support the relational operators: <, <=, > and >=.

In the above list of operators, and O stand for the

complexity, In short, though complexity means the time and/or space complexity of the function, in containers it is the time complexity;

- O(1) stands for constant-time complexity;
- O(log n) stands for logarithm-time complexity;
- O(n) stands for linear-time complexity;

in comparison, O(n) > O(log n) > O(1), which means O(1) is the fastest operation; and caution: These are expected, or average complexity, and the Standard Library document quotes worst-case complexities for some of the operators.

There are a few containers which do not support iterators, and they are: container adapters, bitset, and valarray. Note: C++11 defines iterators begin () and end () for the valarray.

STL Iterators

Iterators, containers, and algorithms are components of the Standard Template Library written by Alexander Stepanov et al., of Hewlett-Packard in the early 1990s and subsequently merged and advanced in the Standard Library.

An iterator is an abstraction of a specialized pointer that dereferences over elements of a given container (such as vector, map, and user made container classes).

Each container class would contain member

functions for generating iterators, for example, members begin (), and end () would return iterator for the first element, and for one after its last element, respectively.

The following figure depicts the relation between an iterator (*it) and its container (vector<int>data {1111, 1134, 1134, 1124, 1124, 1134, 1111, 1176, 1124, 1134, 1176}).

Then, the iterator can incorporate those elements of the container in algorithmic operations (such as sort, accumulate, and user made algorithm functions).

In other words, an iterator associates a container with an algorithm.

The most frequently used iterators are from begin () and end (). This is illustrated in the figure below:

As shown in the figure, both data [0] and data. begin() represent the same element, i.e., elem 1, but data[N] and data.end() represent a "no man land" and accessing this can cause a runtime error. However, the member function end () is very useful in making conditions in iterative statements.

The following code illustrates this fundamental property of iterators:

```
// iterators.cpp

#include "..\..\my_essentials.hpp"
```

```cpp
void illustrate iterators()

{

int arr[] = {1111, 1134, 1134, 1124, 1124, 1134, 1111, 1176, 1124, 1134, 1176};

vector<int>data(arr, arr+ sizeof(arr)/sizeof(arr[0]) );

// vector<int>data2{1111, 1134, 1134, 1124, 1124, 1134, 1111, 1176, 1124, 1134, 1176}; // fine with gcc4.7.0

cout   << "\n Illustration of iterators: \n"

    << "\n Given vector: data =\n\t( ";

for(auto element: data) // 'the range-based for' do not work with VC10.

    cout << element << "; ";

cout << ")\n\n Let us define an iterator, say *it for this vector.\n";

vector<int>::iterator it = data.begin();

/*

Note:

In STL containers, each container template class

defines its own iterator member class, so that

vector<int>::iterator is different from the

list <int>::iterator.

*/

cout << " Thus,\t\t*it = " << *it << " that is data[0]\n Iterators can be incremented, i.e, ++it;\n";

++it;

cout << " After ++\t*it = " << *it << " that is data[1]\n Therefore, iterator *it dereferences through vector data.\n So, let us
```

```cpp
for(auto it = data.begin(); it!=data.end(); ++it)

    cout << *it << "; ";

cout << ")\n";

cout << "\n Task: Since, this vector has repeated numbers,\n
Can we keep only one copy of each number and remove the
duplicates?\n Yes, we can!\n For that, we pass the iterator
through three type of STL algorithms as shown below:\n";

cout << "\n Step.1 Sort in ascending order:\n";

sort(data.begin(), data.end());

cout << " After the iterator has passed through sort(): \n\t( ";

for(auto element: data)

    cout << element << "; ";

cout << ")\n\n Step.2 Move the adjacent repeated elements to
the left hand side:\n";

auto my_unique = unique(data.begin(), data.end());

cout << " After the iterator has passed through unique(): \n\t( ";

for(auto element: data)

    cout << element << "; ";

/*

The function unique() has returned an iterator to

the identifier "my_unique" starting from which the

repeated elements are pushed up to one before the

end().

Note: The STL algorithms can displace the elements

but it cannot erase them, however each stl container
```

template class has a member function called

"erase()" operation for erasing the specified

elements.

In other words, iterators can modify elements in containers but not the containers themselves.

Therefore, to remove the duplicates, we apply the

operation erase() from the iterator "my unique" till

the end().

```cpp
*/
cout << ")\n\n Step.3 Erase out those repeated elements:\n";

data.erase(my unique, data.end());

cout << " After the iterator has passed through erase() i.e., \n Final:\t( ";

for(auto element: data)

    cout << element << "; ";

cout << ")\n";

}
int main()

{
 illustrate_iterators();

 just_pause();

}
```

Output:

Illustration of iterators:

Given vector: data =

(1111; 1134; 1134; 1124; 1124; 1134; 1111; 1176; 1124; 1134; 1176;)

Let us define an iterator, say *it for this vector.

Thus,   *it = 1111 that is data[0].

Iterators can be incremented, i.e, ++it.

After ++   *it = 1134 that is data[1]

Therefore, iterator *it dereferences through vector data.

So, let us express the entire vector using the iterator:

(1111; 1134; 1134; 1124; 1124; 1134; 1111; 1176; 1124; 1134; 1176;)

Task: Since, this vector has repeated numbers,

Can we keep only one copy of each number and remove the duplicates?

Yes, we can!

For that, we pass the iterator through three types of STL algorithms as shown below:

Step.1 Sort in ascending order:

After the iterator has passed through sort():

(1111; 1111; 1124; 1124; 1124; 1134; 1134; 1134; 1134; 1176; 1176;)

Step.2 Move the adjacent repeated elements to the left hand side:

After the iterator has passed through unique():

(1111; 1124; 1134; 1176; 1124; 1134; 1134; 1134; 1134; 1176; 1176;)

Step.3 Erase out those repeated elements:

After the iterator has passed through erase() i.e.,

Final: (1111; 1124; 1134; 1176;)

The program presented above demonstrates the usefulness of iterators incorporating container data in algorithms.

As we saw, the iterators can be used for printing the contents of a container, so let us code a container-independent code in our header file "my_essentials.hpp". This is for easy printing of containers of one type name such as vector<T>, list<T>, set<T>, multiset<T>, deque<T> and fixed-size array<T,N>, but not for containers with two type names such as map<T1,T2> and unordered_multimap<T1,T2>.

```
//-------------------------------------------------
// Container independent code for printing out
// container with one typename
template<typename container>
```

void cout_container(const std::string& message, const container& data)

```cpp
{
    std::cout << message << "{";
    if(data.empty()){
        std::cout << "NULL}"<<std::endl;
        return;
    }
    auto start = data.begin();
    auto end = data.end();
    while(true)
    {
        std::cout << *start;
        ++start;
        if(start != end)
            std::cout << ", ";
        else{
            std::cout <<'}' << std::endl;
            break;
        }
    }
}
```

//--

Let us add this template in the "my_essentials.hpp" and test the template with the following code.

Then, let us test this template:

```cpp
// cout_containers.cpp
#include "..\..\my_essentials.hpp"
#include <array>
#include <vector>
#include <unordered_set>
#include <forward_list>
#include <set>
int main()
{
    // Let us define,
    // a fixed-size array
    array<int,6> arr = {1,3,5,1,2,4};
    cout_container("my array\t = ", arr);

    // a vector
    vector<int> vec(arr.begin(), arr.end());
    cout_container("my vector\t = ", vec);
    // a forward_list
    forward_list<int>
        f_lis(arr.begin(), arr.end());
    cout_container("my forward_list\t = ",f_lis);
```

```
// an unordered_set
unordered_set<int>
    u_set(arr.begin(), arr.end());
cout_container("my unordered_set = ", u_set);
// a set container
set<int>se(arr.begin(), arr.end());
cout_container("my set\t\t = ", se);
just_pause();

}
```

The output is:

my array   = {1, 3, 5, 1, 2, 4}

my vector   = {1, 3, 5, 1, 2, 4}

my forward_list = {1, 3, 5, 1, 2, 4}

my unordered_set = {1, 3, 5, 2, 4}

my set   = {1, 2, 3, 4, 5}

As we experimented with some applications of iterators, now we summarize their operations in the following table.

Iterators do not have a single definition, so not all iterators can support every operation mentioned above. Iterators are categorized into five kinds, viz.

Thus, with this primary discussion, we found that pointers and their property of dereferencing over different objects play a vital role to iterators and STL operations.

CHAPTER - 7
STL ALGORITHM

The STL algorithms are found in <algorithms> header file, so we need to include it in our program.

The algorithms can be classified as:

- Non-modifying algorithms: e.g. for each, count, search etc.

- Modifying algorithms: e.g copy, transform, etc.

- Removing algorithms: remove, remove if, etc.

- Mutating algorithms: reverse, rotate, etc.

- Sorting algorithms: sort, partial sort, etc.

- Sorted range algorithms: binary search, merge, etc.

- Numeric algorithms: accumulate, partial sum, inner product, etc.

The following example shows how to sort () function works on arrays.

Program 13.11: sorting of array using sort algorithm

#include <iostream>

#include <algorithm>

using namespace std;

```cpp
int main()
{
    int a[ ] = {3,5,7,2,9};
    sort(a, a + 5);
    cout << "Sorted Array:" << endl;
    for (int i = 0; i <5; i++)
        cout << a[i] << " ";
    return 0;
}
```

Output:

Sorted Array:

2 3 5 7 9

In the example above, when we pass array name an as an argument, we are telling the function, to sort at the beginning of the array. If we wanted it to start the sort at the third element of the array, we can use,

sort(a+3, a+5);

We have used a+5 for the second argument, which

specifies that we want to sort to the last element in the array.

Now similar sort() function can work with vector container as shown in following program. This shows that STL algorithms are generic.

Program 13.12: Sorting of vector using sort algorithm

#include <iostream>

#include <algorithm>

#include <vector>

using namespace std;

```
int main()
{
    int a[ ] = {5,3,7,6,2,9};
    vector<int> v(a, a+6) ;
    sort(v.begin(), v.end());
    for (int i = 0; i != v.size(); i++)
        cout << v[i] << " ";
    cout << endl;
    return 0;
}
```

Output: 2 3 5 6 7 9

As you can see, the sorting function works almost the same as on an array. The first parameter in sort() accepts an iterator to the first element using begin() as it returns a iterator to the first element. So it will start sorting at the first element in the vector. Same way end() returns an iterator that points to 1 past the last element in the container. Note that sort function sorts up to but not including what we pass as the second parameter.

find() and count() algorithm

find() algorithm is helpful to find particular value from the container. count() is used to count how many times a particular value appears in container.

Program 13.13: Finding value from vector using find algorithm

```cpp
#include <iostream>
#include <algorithm>
#include <vector>
using namespace std;
```

```cpp
int main()
{
vector<int> v;
for(int i = 0; i < 10; i++)
v.push_back(i);
int a = 5;
vector<int>::iterator it;
```

```
it = find(v.begin(),v.end(),a);

if(it != v.end()) {

cout << "found " << a<< endl;

}

else {

cout << "could not find " << a << endl;

}

int c = count(v.begin(), v.end(), 6);

    cout<<"Number of 6 stored in vector:" << c;

return 0;

}
```

Output: found 5

Number of 6 stored in vector: 1

- For each()

This algorithm applies a specified function object to each element in a container. Original values in container will not change, but it is used for display modified elements. It takes the first two arguments as the start and end range. The third argument is an address of a function object.

For example, for each() algorithm squares all elements of the array and displays them.

Program 13.14: To square all elements of array using for each algorithm

```cpp
#include <iostream>

#include <vector>

#include <algorithm>

using namespace std;

void square(int a)
{
    cout<<a*a<<endl;
}
int main()
{
int s[ ]={1,2,3,4};
for_each(s, s+4, square);
return 0;
}
```

Output:

1

4

9

16

CHAPTER - 8

LIBRARY FUNCTIONS

Library functions and user-defined functions in C++

Learning objective

After completing this topic, you should be able to give a brief account of library functions and user-defined functions in C++.

1. Incorporation of library functions

The C++ programmer has access to a large selection of library functions.

You can use any function in the library by simply including the name of the header file that contains the appropriate function prototype.

Generally, library functions are specified in a pair of files.

The function definition is contained in a source file that usually has a .c or .cpp file extension.

Note

Usually, you are not supplied with the source code for library functions with a compiler.

Instead, you are supplied with precompiled object files that can be linked to your program.

The function prototype is contained in a header file, which may be distinguished by an .h, .hpp, or .hxx file extension.

Note

Header files also contain definitions of various data types and constants needed by those functions.

Though not mandatory, it's a good idea to organize your own functions in the same way as supplied library functions.

This allows you to use the functions in more than one program without having to respecify the code.

In order to call library functions in a program, you must specify the header file that contains the appropriate function prototype.

This is usually done at the beginning of a source file.

But it must be done before the function is used by the program.

Header files can be included in a program by using the #include preprocessor directive.

This tells the preprocessor to open the named header file and insert its contents where the #include statement appears.

#include <string>

#include "myfuncs.h"

You can name files in an #include statement in two ways, that is in double quotes or in angle brackets (<>).

Filenames in angle brackets tell the preprocessor to look through a search path specified in the environment.

#include <string>

#include "myfuncs.h"

Filenames in double quotes tell the preprocessor to search the current directory first, then the specified search path.

An error is reported if a file cannot be found.

#include <string>

#include "myfuncs.h"

The linker always searches for the compiled versions of any functions specified in an included header file.

Available files

The C standard library provides a collection of functions for performing common tasks such as:

- String handling
- Character and type conversion
- Mathematics
- Input and output

A wide variety of C++ library files are also available.

The ANSI standard for C++ libraries was ratified in 1998.

The iostream file is probably the most common and generic of all C++ library files.

Most C++ programs include this header file.

The iostream file provides a large range of input/output functions and other I/O stream information.

For example, this is where cin and cout data and functions are prototyped.

Note

C++ I/O occurs in streams of bytes, where a stream is simply a sequence of bytes.

There are many variations of C++ libraries available to programmers.

And these libraries originate from a number of sources.

For example, some libraries come with C++ application development software.

C++ function libraries may also be supplied by sources such as device driver manufacturers, and C++ programming web sites and bulletin boards.

Your best source of reference is usually the manuals and help files included with your C++ application development software.

There are also a number of reference books available, some of which cover specific compilers.

Use of library functions

To demonstrate the use of standard library functions, let's consider a program that does the following:

- Gets the absolute value of the number -55

```
#include <iostream>

using namespace std;

#include <cmath>

void main(void)

{

  cout <<"The absolute value of -55 is "<<abs(-55)<< "\n";
```

- Calculates the square root of 100

calculates the square root of 100

```
cout <<"The square root of 100 is "<<sqrt(100.0)<<
"\n";
```

- evaluates 10 to the power of 5

evaluates 10 to the power of 5

```
cout<<"10 to the power of 5 is"<<pow(10, 5)<< "\n";
```

The result of each calculation is output to the screen.

Note

This program uses no user-defined functions.

The standard math library contains functions to perform each of the three calculations required.

These are:

- abs()

- sqrt()

- pow()

pow()

```
#include <iostream>
```

```
using namespace std;
```

```
#include <cmath>
```

```
void main(void)

{

    cout <<"The absolute value of -55 is "<<abs(-55)<< "\n";

    cout <<"The square root of 100 is "<<sqrt(100.0)<< "\n";

    cout <<"10 to the power of 5 is "<<pow(10,5)<< "\n";

}
```

The first thing to decide when writing this program is which header files to include.

To call abs(), sqrt(), and pow(), you need to include the header file cmath in a preprocessor directive.

You also need to include the header file iostream so that cin and cout statements can be used.

#include <iostream>

using namespace std;

#include <cmath>

```
void main(void)

{

    cout <<"The absolute value of -55 is "<<abs(-55)<< "\n";

    cout <<"The square root of 100 is "<<sqrt(100.0)<< "\n";

    cout <<"10 to the power of 5 is "<<pow(10,5)<< "\n";

}
```

Note

The function abs() is also included in the stdlib.h header file.

Once you've completed the preprocessor directives, you can begin coding main().

#include <iostream>

using namespace std;

#include <cmath>

```cpp
void main(void)
{
    cout <<"The absolute value of -55 is "<<abs(-55)<< "\n";
    cout <<"The square root of 100 is "<<sqrt(100.0)<< "\n";
    cout <<"10 to the power of 5 is "<<pow(10,5)<< "\n";
}
```

statements.

You can display a combination of constants, data types, and expression values in a cout statement, provided that each unique item is separated by the insertion operator (<<).

#include <iostream>

using namespace std;

#include <cmath>

```
void main(void)

{

    cout <<"The absolute value of -55 is "<<abs(-55)<< "\n";

    cout <<"The square root of 100 is "<<sqrt(100.0)<< "\n";

    cout <<"10 to the power of 5 is "<<pow(10,5)<< "\n";

}
```

In the first cout statement, the first value displayed is a constant string.

Then the return value of the math library function abs() is displayed through a call to the function.

#include <iostream>

using namespace std;

#include <cmath>

```
void main(void)

{

    cout <<"The absolute value of -55 is "<<abs(-55)<< "\n";

    cout <<"The square root of 100 is "<<sqrt(100.0)<< "\n";

    cout <<"10 to the power of 5 is "<<pow(10,5)<< "\n";

}
```

The abs() function calculates the absolute value of the integer passed as its function parameter. And the function returns a value of type int.

In this example the argument is a constant, instead of a variable of type int.

#include <iostream>

using namespace std;

#include <cmath>

```cpp
void main(void)
{
  cout <<"The absolute value of -55 is "<<abs(-55)<< "\n";
  cout <<"The square root of 100 is "<<sqrt(100.0)<< "\n";
  cout <<"10 to the power of 5 is "<<pow(10,5)<< "\n";
}
```

When the cout statement is executed, the function is called, and the number 55 is displayed on screen.

#include <iostream>

using namespace std;

#include <cmath>

```cpp
void main(void)
{
  cout <<"The absolute value of -55 is "<<abs(-55)<< "\n";
  cout <<"The square root of 100 is "<<sqrt(100.0)<< "\n";
  cout <<"10 to the power of 5 is "<<pow(10,5)<< "\n";
}
```

The next two lines of code perform function calls in

the same way as the first line.

The function sqrt() accepts a single argument of type double and returns a value of type double.

In this example, the number 10 is displayed on screen.

#include <iostream>

using namespace std;

#include <cmath>

```cpp
void main(void)
{
    cout <<"The absolute value of -55 is "<<abs(-55)<< "\n";
    cout <<"The square root of 100 is "<<sqrt(100.0)<< "\n";
    cout <<"10 to the power of 5 is "<<pow(10,5)<< "\n";
}
```

Note

A domain error occurs if the argument is a negative number.

The library function pow() accepts two arguments of type double and returns a value of type double.

When the cout statement executes, the number 100000 is displayed.

#include <iostream>

using namespace std;

#include <cmath>

```cpp
void main(void)
{
    cout <<"The absolute value of -55 is "<<abs(-55)<< "\n";
    cout <<"The square root of 100 is "<<sqrt(100.0)<< "\n";
    cout <<"10 to the power of 5 is "<<pow(10,5)<< "\n";
}
```

CHAPTER - 9

I/O

I/O basic

I/O basic knowledge

- Neither C++ nor C has built input and output in the language. They use functions(C) or other I/O obje cts (C++) in language library.

- C++ I/O class and head file

1. Iofs stand for three head files <iostream> <fstream> and <sstream>. <iostream> includes <ios> automatically. They are three main header file you should include in your C++ application.

2. Classes: iostream(streambuf), fstream(filebuf), stringstream(stringbuf) and four pre-defined object: cin, cout, clog and cerr

3. Clog is just like cerr, but it buffer its output.

4. C++ normally flushes the input buffer when you press enter. For output to the display, C++ program normally flushes the output buffer

when you transmit a newline character, or reaches an input statement.

5. >> And << don't need to format string, C++ will automatically, convert it, it's better than printf and scanf in C language.

6. Through inheritance, fstream and cin(cout) share the same usage. All the knowledge can be used directly in fstream. I like it the most.

Input

Input basic knowledge

- For Input, you need to master one basic idea, two languages, and three data type.

- One basic idea: In order to make continuously input, you need to use while(inputMethod), When two things happens:

1. User want to end input(ctrl+D) or read the end of File;

2. Read fail (for example, cin>> int, but input letter 'a'),

InputMethod will return false. Then you need to use some flag or status to tell the difference between EOF and error inside of while loop.

- Two languages is c and c++, they use the different inputMethod. three data types are: number and word(no space in middle), character(white), and string(include space in middle)

- Two languages common used input method
- Number and non-white character word Character (including white-character) string(line)

C   scanf("%d %f %c %s",&i, &f,&c);

int a = getchar();   fgets(stdin, char*p, n)

C++   cin>>i>>f>>c>>w;   cin.get(char & c);

Ch = cin.get();   cin.get(char *p, n);

cin.getline(char *p, n);

getline(cin, string);

- In scanf, you need to specify exact data type when you read.

1. H: short int or short unsigned. Example: %hd or %hu.

2. I: a long int or long unsigned, or double (for %f conversions.) Example: %ld, %lu, or %lf.

3. L: The value to be parsed is a long for integer types or long double for float types. Example: %Ld, %Lu, or %Lf.

4. *: Tells scanf() do to the conversion specified, but not store it anywhere. This is what you use if you want scanf() to eat some data, but you don't want to store it anywhere; you don't give scanf() an argument for this conversion. Example: %*d.

- Scanf("%c" &c) will read any character, including whitespace character. If you want to scanf skip any whitespace, you can use space before %c.

1. While(true){

2. Scanf("%c",&c);

3. //scanf(" %c",&c);

4. Printf("you_input:_%d" c);

5. }

Output:

When you input a(enter), output will be like you input: 97(a value) you input: 10(enter value)

- cin>>c will not read white character(tab, space , newline), If you want to read them from input buffer, You should use getchar() or cin.get(); If you want the user to input his or her name.

1. While(true){

2. Cin>>c;

3. Cout<<"you_input:"<<c<<endl;

4. }

Output:

When you input " a(enter)" output will be like:you input: a. then cursor wait for here.

- Using cin>> or scanf will terminate the string

after it reads the first space. The best way to handle this situation is to use the function to read a line;

1. Read word and line:

2. Scanf(%s,char_array) //c

3. Cin>>char_array or ; //c++

4. Cin>> str;

5. //line

6. Gets(char_array) //c

7. Fgets(char_array, n , FILE *)

8. Cin.getline(char * ,int n)

9. Cin.get(char * ,int n)

10. Std::getline(istream& is, string& str)

Line 1: Read a word until reach white character.

Line 7: Recommend to use this for safety.

Line 9: C++ read and discard newline

Line 1: Not read newline

- Cin.read function has the same interface with cin.get, but it doesn't append a null character to input, It's not intend for keyboard input, but for binary format of file

- For C++, three get, two getline, other use >>;

- Difference between cin.get(char) and int = cin.get()

1. while(cin.get(c))

2. // use cin.get(char) in reading loop

3. cin.get() != '\n'

4. //use cin.get() return character to test sth.

5. cin.get()!= EOF

Line 7: When used in EOF, you have to use int. because EOF may not be expressed by char type

- Confused functions: cin.get and cin.getline are almost the same things.

Cin.get (char* s, streamsize n, char delim);

Cin.getline (char* s, streamsize n, char delim);

Istream& getline (istream& is, string& str);

1. For each line, if you don't know the max length, just use getline(cin, string). You don't need to input any length. (you can reserve length of string if you want to avoid allocation of memory)

2. cin.get() doesn't discard delim from input stream. However, cin.getline() will read and discard newline. (It's easy for you to remember, because, line is defined by newline character)

3. In cin.getline(char* s, int n) The failbit flag is set if the function extracts no characters(newline

is a character), Or if the delimiting character is not found once (n-1) characters have already been written to s. Note that if the character that follows those (n-1) characters in the input sequence is precisely the delimiting character, it is also extracted and the failbit flag is not set.

4. In.cin.get(char* s , int n). The failbit flag is set only if the function extracts no characters.

5. cin.get(char* s, n) is more flexible than cin. getline. Because when it read to the array is full, It doesn't set failbit. At this time you can use gcount() or peek() to see if the next character is a new line. It's more customized than cin.getline();

Input Pattern

- It is a bad idea to test the stream on the outside and then read/write to it inside the body of the conditional/loop statement. This is because the act of reading may make the stream bad. It is usually better to do the read as part of the test.

while(!cin.fail()){ // that is bad programming style

cin>>i; //here may make stream fail().

.....   //then i is not valid value

}

- If you just want to input, you don't want to know eof or deal with failbit. You can use below:

```
while(scanf("%d",&i) != 1)

while((int c = getchar())!=EOF)

while( fgets(line, sizeof(line), fp) != NULL )

//in c language, use these to exit loop!

while(cin>>input)

while(cin.get(p, 20) )

while(getline(ifstream, string)) {

//in C++ language, use bool operator to exit loop.

//do some useful things.  //input is right.

}
```

- If you want to know eof or deal with the error. You can use the below code. When you press enter, the read will end. When you input letter, it will get rid of this letter until you input number.

```
1. while(true) //use break to exit loop;
2. {
3. cin>>i//or getline(ifstream, string);
4. If(cin.eof()){  //If it's EOF
5. cout<<"EOF_encountered"<<endl
6. //break;
7. }
```

```
8. If(cin.fail()) //deal with Invalide input
9. {
10. cin.clear(); //Important. clear state and buffer
11. while(cin.get()!='\n')  //get rid rest of line,
12. continue ;
13. cout<<"please_input_a_number"<<endl;
14. continue;
15. }
16. ... // input is right.do some useful things.
17.}
```

- In the previous example, why do we need to distinguish eof and fail? When fail happen, maybe there are invalid character in buffer. After clean the buffer, I can continue to read input from input buffer. Three methods to clean invalid character in the buffer.

```
cin.clear();   //Important. clear state and buffer
while(cin.get()!='\n')
continue ;      // method 1
while(!issapce(cin.get()))
continue;  //method 2
basic_istream& ignore(streamsize _Count = 1, \
int_type _Delim = traits_type::eof()); //method 3
```

```
cin.ignore(5, 'a');

cin.ignore(numeric_limits<streamsize>::max(), '\n');
```

- You can use istream_iterator, It can save you some trouble to judge EOF.

1. Class A{

2. Private:

3. Int x,y;

4. Friend istream& operator>>(istream& in, A&);

5. Friend ostream& operator<<(ostream& in, const A&);

6. };

7. istream& operator>>(istream& in, A& a){

8. In>>a.x>>a.y;

9. return in;

10. }

11. Ostream& operator<<(ostream& out, const A& a){

12. Out<<a.x<< "_" <<a.y;

13. Return out;

14. }

15. Vector<A> v;

16. Copy(istream_iterator<A>(cin),istream_iterator<A>(),

17. Back_inserter(v));

18. Copy(v.begin(),v.end(),ostream iterator<A>(cout, "\n"));

- In summary, its better just use judgment to exit end loop. If you need to different specific action to take to deal with EOF or error. Use while(true), then use eof() of feof() fail() or clear() functions in c++ and c to deal with and break the loop;

Output:

- For cout, It can recognize type automatically, and It is extensible, you can redefine << operator so that cout can recognize you data type.

1. Class Foo{

2. Friend ostream & operator<<(ostream& s,const Foo &r);

3. 3.}

4. Ostream & operator<<(ostream& s, const Foo &r){

5. 6. S<<Foo.a<<Foo.b<<endl;

6. 7.}

- How to print pointer address in C and C++?

char* amount = "dozen";

cout<< amount ; //print "dozen" string

```
cout<<(void*) amount;//prints the address of pointer
```

```
printf("%p", (void*) p);
```

- Format is key point for Output. You need to know the common manipulator to control the output format.

- Number base manipulators: hex, oct and dec; Field widths: Width, fill, precision Setf()

- You don't need to know the details, just name of them. When you want to use them, go to reference website to look. A detail format manipulators can be seen on C++ primer P1090. You need to include <iomanip>

- << is a bitwise left-shift operator in C language, but in C++, we overloaded it in ostream class, cout is an object of ostream,

- You can use cout<<flush to force flushing the output buffer

- cout.write can be used to output a string; It will output certain length string, even reach the end of string.

Other stream

File

- When you studied cin and cout very well, you will find that file operation is so easy. Just change cin or cout to your ifstream , ofstream or fstream object.

```cpp
std::fstream ifs;

ifs.open ("test.txt", ios_base::in| ios_base::binary);

if(!ifs.is_open())

  exit(1);

char c = ifs.get();

// use all previous input methods

ifs.close();
```

- Only read ifsteam; only write ofsteam; write and read fstream.

- For ios_base::binary mode, use write() and read() function.

- For writing, pay attention to the difference between ios_base:: trunc and ios_base:: app

- Random access is used mostly on binary file. Because the position can be pinpointed exactly. For seekg() for input, and seekp() for output.(p is put, g is get) It moves the pointer. tellp() and tellg() function. It tells the position of pointer.

Buffer and string buffer

- Stringstream is a convenient way to manipulate strings like an independent I/O device. Sometimes it is very convenient to use stringstream to convert between strings and other numerical types. The usage of stringstream are much the same with iostream, so it is not a burden to learn.

- You need to build a stringstream from a string, or convert a stringstream back to a string.

1. stringstream outstr;

2. outstr<<"salary_value"<<123333.00<<endl;

3. string str = outstr.str() //change to string

4. istringstream Instr(str);

5. while(instr>>number)

6. cout<<number<<endl

7. char sentence []="Yan_is_41_years_old";

8. char str [20];

9. int i;

10. sscanf (sentence,"%s_%*s_%d", str, &i);

11. sprintf(...);

Line 1 to 3: Change number to a text.

Line 5 to 7: Change text to a number.

Line 9 to end: C language method. In line 12, you can see "*s", it means input will be ignored. So str = Yan, i = 41.

Manipulate stream

1. Peek return the next character from input without extracting from the input stream. For

example, you want to read input up to the first newline or period.

```
char input[80];

int i = 0;

while( (ch=cin.peek()) != '.' && ch != '\n')

  cin.get(input[i++];)

input[i] = '\0';
```

2. Gcount() method returns the number of characters read by the last unformatted extraction method. That means character read by the a get(), getline(), ignore(), or read(), but not extraction operator.

3. Putback() function inserts a character back in the input buffer.

CHAPTER - 10
MEMORY AND RESOURCES

Memory Management

C++ programming language provides a lot of options to users when it comes to managing the memory used by an executing program. In this chapter, we shall be exploring some of these frequently used options. We would also introduce some modern techniques aimed at reducing the memory management problems that have plagued C++ projects in the past.

Memory Available to C++ Programs

Modern operating systems usually reserve a section of its memory for executing a program that allows the operating system to manage multiple program executions simultaneously. There are different operating systems which layout the memory of executing the program in different ways. However, the layout would include the following four sections.

- Code: The program's compiled executable

instructions are held in the code section memory. While the program executes, the contents of the code section should never change. Also, during the program's executions, the code segment does not change as well.

- Data: Persistent variables and global variables are held in the data section of the memory as in static locals. Throughout the life span of the executing program is the variables of the data would exist. However, unless the data is a constant, the executing program may freely change their values. Although the values stored in the variables found in the data segment may change during the program's execution, the size of the data segment wouldn't change while the program is executing. It is so because the program's source code precisely defines the numbers of global and static local variables. It is also possible for the compiler to compute the exact size of the data segment.

- Heap: The section where the executing program obtains dynamic memory is called the heap. Using the new operator gets the memory from the heap, and the delete operator returns the previously allocated memory back to the heap. The size of the heap shrinks and fries during the program's execution as the program deallocates and allocates dynamic memory using the delete and new.

- Stack: Function parameters and local variables

are always stored in the stack. Function parameters and local variables disappear when the function returns and appears when a function is called. The size of the stack also shrinks and grows during the program's execution as various functions execute.

Generally, operating systems limit the size of the stack. Deep recursion can consume a considerable amount of stack space. For example, let's consider an improperly written recursive function of one that omits the base case and thus exhibits an "infinite" recursion that would consume all the space that is available on the stack. A situation such as this is known as a stack overflow. Modern operating systems terminate any process that consumes a lot of the stack space. However, on some embedded systems, this stack overflow may go undetected. Typically, heap space is plentiful, and operating systems can use virtual memory to provide more space than it's available in real memory for an executing program. The extra space for the virtual memory comes from a disk drive, and the operating system shuttles data from the disk to real memory as needed by the executing program. Programs that make use of a virtual memory run a lot more slowly than programs that make use of little virtual memory.

Manual Memory Management

Frequent memory management issues with delete and new are the majorly difficult to find and fix the source of the logic error. Programmers have to adhere strictly to the following tenets:

- Everything you call new, it should always have an associated call to delete provided the allocated memory isn't longer needed. It may sound simple, but it isn't always clear when delete should be used, but the function below shows a memory leak:

```
void calc(int n) {
// ...
// Do some stuff
// ...
int *x = new int[n];
// ...
// Do some stuff with x
// ...
// Exit function without deleting x's memory
}
```

Provided a program calls on the calc function enough times, the program will eventually run out of memory. In the calc function, x is a local variable. In that light, x lives on the stack. So when a user uses a particular call to calc completes, the function's clean up code automatically releases the space helped by the variable x. Because all functions automatically manage the memory for their local and parameter variables. The problem with x is assigned via new to point to memory allocated from the heap and not the stack. Function executions manage to which x pointed is no deallocated automatically.

- Then operator delete should never be used to free up memory that has not been allocated from its previous call to new. The code fragment below illustrates one such example:

```
int list[10], *x = list; // x points to list

// ...

// Do some stuff

// ... delete [ ] x; // Logic error, attempt to deallocate x's
memory
```

The space references by the pointer x were not allocated by the operator new, so the operator delete should not be used to attempt to free the memory. When you attempt to delete a memory that is not allocated with new, it results in an undefined behavior that proves a logic error.

- The operator delete must not be used to deallocate the same memory more than once. This case is common when two pointers refer to the same memory. Pointers like this are called aliases. The following code fragment below illustrates this situation better:

```
int *p = new int[10], *y = x; // y aliases x
// ...
// Do some stuff with x and/or y
// ...
delete [ ] x; // Free up x's memory
// ...
// Do some other stuff
// ...
delete [ ] y; // Logic error, y's memory already freed!
```

Since the pointer x and pointer y point to the same memory, then x and y are aliases of each other. If you deallocate a memory that is referenced by one of them, then the other memory is also deallocated since it is the same memory.

- When you deallocating previous memory with delete, they should never accessed. When you attempt to access deleted memory result, it would result in an undefined behaviors which represent a logical error.

```
int *list = new int[10];
// ... // Use list, then
// ... delete [ ] list;
// Deallocate list's memory
// ... // Sometime later
// ... int x = list[2]; // Logic error, but sometimes works!
```

The code fragment above illustrates how such a situation could arise. For the purpose of efficiency, the delete operator makes heap space as available without modifying the contents in the memory.

Resource Management

It is essential that programmers call clear internationally when they finish with a linked list object. Take a look at the following definition:

```
void x() {
IntList1 my_list; // Constructor called here
// Add some numbers to the list
my_list.insert(12);
my_list.insert(7);
my_list.insert(-14);
// Print the list
my_list.print();
} // Oops! Forgot to call my list.clear!
```

In the code above, the variable my list is local to function x. When the function x finishes executing the variable my list, it will go out of scope. At this stage, the space on the stack-allocated for the local IntList1 variable named my list is reclaimed. Although the list's head-allocated elements space remains, the only access the program can have to the memory is through my list.head, but my list no longer exists. This is a classic example of a memory leak. Observe that none of the classes we have designed so gat apart from the IntList1 have this problem. However, C++ offers a way out for class designers to specify actions that have to occur at the end of an object's lifespan. A constructor that executes a code at the beginning of an object's existence is known as a destructor. A destructor is a special method that executes immediately before the object stops existing. A destructor can also have the same name as its class with a tilde ~ prefix. Additionally, a destructor does not accept arguments. Code 9.2 shows how to add a destructor to a code and also ass the previously suggested optimization of the length and clear methods.

```
Code 9.2
// Code9.2
class Code9.2 {
// The nested private Node class from before
struct Node {
int data; // A data element of the list
Node *next; // The node that follows this one in the list
Node(int d); // Constructor
};
Node *head; // Points to the first item in the list
Node *tail; // Points to the last item in the list
int len; // The number of elements in the list
public:
// The constructor makes an initially empty list
```

```cpp
  IntList2();
// The destructor that reclaims the list's memory

~Code9.2(); // Inserts n onto the back of the list.
void insert(int n);
// Prints the contents of the linked list of integers.
void print() const;
// Returns the length of the linked list.
int length() const;
// Removes all the elements in the linked list.
void clear();
};
```

CONCLUSION

After taking you on a guide on ten of the must-know topics in C++, it is left to you now to develop your skills. And one thing with languages, be in English, French, or programming languages, practice makes perfect. The knowledge we've thought you in this book can be likened to learning the alphabet and some basic words in English. So, we'd advise you to practice with it more. Focus your mind on understanding why we use some statements; the result we want to obtain.

Go online, download all the necessary application that you find easy to work with, and if you'd have to pay for it, purchase it. And when you have everything all set and ready, pick up a project and learn. You could build your own little project, or you could pick an already made project and try to replicate it. If you ever get stuck anywhere, you can always go back, and view and the programmer made the project and proceeded. But always try to push yourself to your limit, think deep about it before checking.

It would also help you a great deal to pick up other really good books to get different perceptions about a section in C++ to broaden your understanding of it. Even though we can assure you of the quality of this book is sufficient to set you on the right path to becoming a success in C++, we would recommend you also read out other books on the programming language.

Also, you could consider picking a different language other than C++ to learn side by side with C++. Leaning a new language is an efficient way to get a more in-depth understanding of C++. A new language brings in better comprehension of the programming language in general. It also broadens your mentality of solving problems, which brings out the specificities of the main C++ language. And even though you may not use this new language codes in C++, it would expose you to proven ideas that you can transpose into C++. A programming language we would advise you to study alongside C++ is Haskell. You can also study Java because it is way closer to our everyday English than C++, and it would be easier for you to understand. You can also check out our book on Java.

Additionally, always try to stay up to date. Catch up with the modern C++ features like C++11, C++14, C++ 17, and a host of other new features in the standard library. Some of its latest features, like lambdas, is easy to grasp. All you need is a good resource and time, and in no time, you'd see yourself becoming a master in them. And so, why not take a cup of tea, find a nice relaxing spot where you find it easier to focus and get started. And just like the famous saying goes, "a journey of a thousand miles begins with a step." So, take that step today, and let us be that guild that will set you on the right path. want to learn how to use it today, then this is the guidebook for you.